Best Practices Guidebook
Professional Learning Communities

Bluegrass Center for Teacher Quality

Matthew B. Courtney, Ed.D.
Joseph Constantine, Ph.D.
Joshua Trosper, M.Ed.

ISBN-13: 978-1548793616
ISBN-10: 1548793612

How to cite this report:
Courtney, M.B., Constantine, J., Trosper, J. (2017). Best Practices Guidebook: Professional Learning Communities. Barbourville, KY . Bluegrass Center for Teacher Quality, Inc.

EXECUTIVE SUMMARY

The Professional Learning Community model of professional growth and development is an increasingly popular method of teacher training. Commonly abbreviated and referred to as PLCs, this style of professional learning is characterized by its focus on small groups and individualized learning. While the PLC has nearly become a standard feature of the American public school, many teachers and administrators have reported difficulty in implementing a meaningful process. By their very nature, PLCs are unique to each school environment, but the research described in this paper suggests that effective PLC processes share a set of common characteristics. This report makes seven best practice recommendations for implementing the professional learning community model.

INTRODUCTION

Within the realm of teaching enhancement, conversations about the role of professional learning communities (PLCs) in schools have become ubiquitous and oftentimes met with a mix of both skepticism and enthusiasm. Advocates of improved professional development for teachers point to decades of educational research highlighting a consensus about effective bases of high-quality learning environments for teachers and students alike. More than ever in history, educators possess a shared vision by which they can empower themselves and their professional counterparts to collaboratively strengthen educational programs that support improved learner outcomes across a range of content areas (Stein, Smith, & Silver, 1999; Hawley & Valli, 1999).

Still, many teachers and administrators have reported challenges with implementation of effective professional learning models at the school and district levels; "where the rubber meets the road." Perhaps unsurprisingly, professional learning communities (PLCs) exist in a wide variety of shapes and sizes with varying degrees of institutional support and efficacy (Grossman et al., 2000, 2001; Shen, Zhen, & Poppink, 2007). More surprising, however, are persistent and widespread questions about the practical needs of PLCs, the nature of activities that drive successful PLC outcomes, and the key elements required to make PLCs doable for teachers and impactful for learners under their tutelage. This report seeks to clearly identify and delineate the critical features of successful PLCs by providing seven recommendations for effective PLCs. Review of relevant educational literature tells us that PLC activities must: be driven by the professionals in the group, foster diversity and collaboration, be framed around a unified vision, be focused on rigorous professional growth, be centered on student achievement and common problems, be informed by peer observations, and be supported by the administration.

SEVEN RECCOMMENDATIONS FOR EFFECTIVE PLCs	
PROFESSIONAL LEARNING COMMUNITIES SHOULD HAVE OWNERSHIP OF THEIR WORK	PROFESSIONAL LEARNING COMMUNITIES SHOULD ENCOURAGE DIVERSITY AND COLLABORATION
PROFESSIONAL LEARNING COMMUNITIES SHOULD HAVE A COMMON VISION	PROFESSIONAL LEARNING COMMUNITIES SHOULD BE FOCUSED ON RIGOROUS PROFESSIONAL GROWTH
PROFESSIONAL LEARNING COMMUNITIES SHOULD FOCUS ON STUDENT OUTCOMES AND COMMON PROBLEMS OF PRACTICE	PROFESSIONAL LEARNNIG COMMUNITITIES SHOULD INCLUDE NON-EVALUATIVE PEER OBSERVATION
PROFESSIONAL LEARNING COMMUNITIES SHOULD HAVE ADEQUATE TIME AND SUPPORT	

RECCOMENDATION ONE

PROFESSIONAL LEARNING COMMUNITIES
SHOULD HAVE OWNERSHIP OF THEIR WORK.

Schools often have an overall perception of what a professional learning community should look like. Many districts purchase PLC handbooks that provide rigid guidelines while state level Departments of Education frame their work through the lens of the professional learning community. Unfortunately, simply adding the letters PLC to the top of an agenda doesn't actually create a learning community (Vescio, Ross, and Adams 2007). In order for a professional learning community to thrive, the individuals involved must have ownership over their work, governance, and participation.

Trust is a key concept in community building and collaborative work. Studies have shown a strong correlation between trust and collaboration; where high levels of trust lead to high levels of collaboration, and vice versa (Demir, 2015; Kallan, 2016). It is important for teachers to be included in the design and implementation of a PLC model. When a PLC process is forced on teachers who have little control in their professional learning, the trust level in the school begins to fall (Whitty 2002, Webb 2009). Gray, Kruse & Tarter (2016) demonstrated that professional learning communities work best in schools with effective PLC structures, a focus on academic achievement, and high levels of collegial trust. By extension, the successful implementation of the PLC supported further development of trust within the school.

When teachers are trusted to work together to solve problems together, the collaborative focus can lead to increased student achievement. A study reported by Englert and Tarrant (1995) demonstrates the importance of teacher authority in the overall success of a learning community. This study explored the efforts of three special education teachers and seven university researchers to provide "meaningful and beneficial" literacy instruction for students with mild disabilities. Even though the teachers each took different approaches to the instruction, their collaborative efforts led to greater understanding and success for the students involved (Englert and Tarrant 1995, Vescio, Ross, and Adams 2007). A similar study in 2012 sought to measure the impact of independent teacher collaborative learning on the development of teacher's self-efficacy. The time spent in thoughtful and deliberate collaborative learning showed increases in their content knowledge and pedagogy, their ability to surpass stated goals, their awareness during peer observation activities, and their ability to provide meaningful feedback (Chong & Kong, 2012).

Administrators and teachers must work together to create PLC procedures that work for their school. This means administrators must trust their teachers to work autonomously, and teachers must trust the best intentions of school administration and reformers. By delegating tasks, the administration is able to build a more knowledgeable and independent faculty base. This, in turn, will help turn the local school from a simplistic hierarchal organization to a complex organization with embedded leadership structures (Bolam et al. 2005, Webb, et al. 2009).

Additionally, teachers must have ownership in the make-up of their PLC groups. Some researchers have gone as far as to suggest that PLC's are ineffective because they do not represent actual primary group community models. Arbitrarily designed, artificial communities lack the social and emotional bonding necessary to effectively collaborate and complete tasks (Vann 1994, 1996). By giving a PLC group ownership over its membership, school administrators can ensure that the groups are able to meet the inter-personal and emotional requirements necessary for collaboration to occur.

RECCOMNDATION TWO

PROFESSIONAL LEARNING COMMUNITIES
SHOULD ENCOURAGE DIVERSITY AND COLLABORATION

Building on the notion that professional learning community members must take ownership over their work, they should also take ownership over their membership. Steps should be taken to ensure that PLC groups respect the diverse needs of the school. While the traditional definition of diversity is applicable here, the makeup of a successful PLC group may include diversity in discipline, grade level, years of experience, or levels of leadership.

The PLC group is strengthened by the content knowledge and experience of each member involved. As such, schools should seek teams of teachers who come from a wide range of perspectives. While work within like-discipline or like-grade level groups can be beneficial in terms of strategic planning and lesson design, interdisciplinary or vertically aligned groups may be more appropriate when trying to solve systemic, school-wide problems. For example, a school working to close achievement gaps in reading or math may benefit from same-discipline, vertically aligned groups that is focused on carrying strategies, common language, or intervention techniques from one grade level to the next, while a school working to solve systemic behavioral issues may benefit from same grade-level, interdisciplinary groups.

Once membership in a group has been decided, each member should commit to collaborating with everyone at the table. Interdisciplinary and inter-level collaboration are key elements to a successful PLC. If the goal of a PLC is to improve the quality of classroom teaching through professional growth and collaboration, then schools must create the expectation that when everyone participates the team helps the individual grow. To put it another way, when the team works to reach its collaborative goal, individual goals are met along the way, leading to overall improvement.

PLC DIVERSITY CATEGORIES
Race/Ethnicity
Religion
Gender
Content Area
Grade Level
Level of Degree Attainment
Years of Experience
Levels of Leadership/Age
Job Category

By extension, each individual PLC team has an impact on the culture of a school. In a 2002 study, Supovitz compared team-based and non-team-based teachers' perceptions of school culture on 33 items that were grouped into five key indicators of school culture. The study found a strong correlation between the experiences of team-based teachers and their perceived involvement in school-related decision making. He concluded that giving teachers the power to be decision makers in their own learning process was essential to improving students' learning. In a similar study, Bolam et al. (2005) demonstrated by harnessing the leadership of strong PLC groups, administrators were better able to develop innovative strategies for use of financial and personnel resources (Supovitz 2002, Bolam et al. 2005).

RECOMMENDATION THREE

PROFESSIONAL LEARNING COMMUNITIES SHOULD HAVE A COMMON VISION

Before a professional learning community can be successful, it must first create a shared and common vision. DuFour and Eaker (1988) clearly lay out this expectation in their initial description of a PLC as a group with a *shared mission, vision, values, and goals*. These four components are required for any type of strategic and meaningful work (Aktan, 2003). As such, it is vital that individuals working together in a PLC have the opportunity to discuss and establish their shared beliefs.

The mission and vision statements refer to the work of the group; describing what they want to accomplish and how they intend to reach their end goal. Most educational institutions have formalized mission and vision statements that guide their work. A review of such statements found that most center on the desire to provide students with a well-rounded and thorough educational experience (Ozdem, 2011). While this goal is admirable for a school as a whole, the mission and vision of the individual PLC group should be focused on the direct needs of the teachers involved in the program.

The values of the group help to describe how the group functions. In fact, to be aligned with any relevant definition of the word community, clearly stated values must be agreed upon (Villa, 2003). Before beginning their work, a new PLC group should spend time discussing the values that will govern and guide their time together. Commonly cited values for school communities include a focus on children, a commitment to democratic decision-making, and the desire to promote the personal and professional growth of each member of the community. This shared sense of value helps to bring people together and focus the work of the group as a whole.

Once these fundamentals of the group have been established, goal setting should become the next priority. There is much debate as to the manner in which educators should set goals. In general, the goal setting process tends to be rooted in some form of data collection and analysis. In the PLC environment, it should also include professional learning goals of the individuals involved.

MISSION	VISION	VALUES
A mission statement states the goals of an organization and how they plan to achieve those goals.	A vision statement states what the world will look like if you have accomplished your goals.	A values statement describes the core principles and values of an organization.

RECCOMENDATION FOUR

PROFESSIONAL LEARNING COMMUNITIES SHOULD BE FOCUSED ON RIGOROUS PROFESSIONAL GROWTH

Although educators are already immersed in a *lesson-driven* environment, PLCs do not necessarily operate with a clear focus on teachers' growth and learning. Reasons for a lack of focus on learning range from weak levels of relational trust to changing administrative expectations and teacher burnout. The end result, however, in many cases, is that PLCs are not easily initiated, nor are they designed in a manner that makes professional development a natural by-product of PLC meetings. In fact, many well-meaning teachers and administrators have reported that they simply do not know how to begin the process of designing high-quality PLC procedures (DuFour, 2011; Louis, 2006).

High-quality PLCs must exhibit an attitude of forward movement, openness to new ideas, self-reflection, and a culture of organizational learning. Preconceived notions about school and classroom operations must be identified and challenged in order to deal with explicit or implicit skepticism about a PLC's ability to generate a change in school culture (Labianca, Gray, & Brass, 2000; Wells & Feun, 2007). In some instances, this process may require an outside facilitator to bring objectivity to the task of creating a progress-centered learning community (Morrissey, 2000).

Beyond cultural and administrative underpinnings, the heart of PLC functionality is the ability of teachers to come together in support of each other's learning. From a practical standpoint, collective teacher efficacy is determined by the quality of collective learning and application of that learning. Participants develop shared values about problems that need to be addressed, engage in reflective dialogue, and embrace de-privatized, (i.e., collaborative) practice. PLC conferences aim to find common ground and a shared vision. At the same time, the PLC plays a pivotal role in promoting individual self-evaluation techniques and personal capacities for refining teaching practices (Lee, Zhang, & Yin, 2011; Owen, 2014; Stoll, Bolam, McMahon, Wallace, & Thompson, 2006). Teachers are able to cooperatively discover programmatic and personal strengths and weaknesses. With this knowledge, teachers can choreograph solution-based strategies that increasingly benefit students. Use of structured conversational and analytical supports can facilitate a strong PLC focus on teaching enhancement (MacBeath, 1999; MacBeath & Mortimore, 2001; MacGilchrist, Myers, & Reed, 2004; Rosenholtz, Bassler, & Hoover-Dempsey, 1986).

Professional learning activities can, furthermore, help eliminate the very barriers that are often thought to impede instructional change (such as teacher burnout and isolation). High-performance PLCs assist in sustaining teachers' commitment to teaching by providing group support, intellectual stimulation, and increased job satisfaction. A focus on learning gives educators access to more dynamic perspectives, elevated understanding of students' thinking, and deeper insights into diverse learners' experiences. Importantly, PLCs can assist in the development of refined metacognitive strategies for teachers, with an emphasis on constructionist-fueled analyses of the ways teachers and students alike build knowledge (individually, as well as with teacher assistance). With a concentration on acquisition of such information, teachers may reap rewards that outweigh investments of time and effort necessary to build strong PLCs: organization into instructional teams, shared success, creation of school-specific systematic interventions, assessment of collective effectiveness, and built-in continuous improvement (DuFour, 2007; Johnson, et al., 2004; Little, 2006; Prytula, 2012).

Without doubt, the most effective forms of professional development are integrated into teachers' daily work, fostering informal and formal learning opportunities for teachers that take place spontaneously throughout the school day (Garet, Porter, Desimone, Birman, & Yoon, 2001; Ingvarson et al., 2005; Schrum & Levin, 2013).

One of the barriers to a successful PLC is a potential lack of intellectual stimulation. Learning communities can, all too often, suffer from *comfortable collaboration* (Hargreaves, 2001), a condition whereby teachers do not challenge each other professionally or cerebrally. Effective PLCs, as stated earlier, need to be highly collaborative. Moreover, PLC participants benefit from setting aside a mindset of isolated practice and seeing the value of *interdependency*. Schools require an atmosphere of progress-bound collaboration with an intellectual focus on daily activities that promote shared responsibilities, e.g., team-teaching. Critical and reflective discussions are desired. Open learning spaces where teachers can regularly and easily see each other at work are ideal. School staff members engage in a *continuous cycle of learning* as they inquire together about interesting topics revolving around student achievement (Sigudardottir, 2010). Many educators find DuFour's (2004) *guiding questions* for teachers useful in this pursuit: *1) What do we want each student to learn? 2) How will we know when each student has learned it? 3) How will we respond when a student experiences difficulty in learning?*

DUFOUR'S GUIDING QUESTIONS		
What do we want each student to learn?	How will we know when each student has learned it?	How will we respond when a student experiences difficulty in learning?

A spirit of collective inquiry is critical to sustaining impactful PLCs. Contributors to the process dedicate themselves to investigating best practices as well as best resources for their growth and development as teachers. While PLC members may seek help from outside experts and mentors, the educators themselves are responsible for becoming passionately engaged in learning. Learning groups/communities support investigations into practical matters, methods of instruction, and strategies for dealing with the day-to-day challenges of teaching. Thoughtful analysis of critical pedagogical issues, such as going beyond *teaching to the test* in an era of intense accountability, fuels teacher commitment to the process. PLCs can, indeed, be a fertile forum for imaginative endeavors that achieve *out of the box* interventions for all kinds of learners (D'Ardenne et.al., 2013; Hoaglund, Birkenfield, & Box, 2014).

RECCOMENDATION FIVE

PROFESSIONAL LEARNING COMMUNITIES SHOULD FOCUS ON STUDENT OUTCOMES AND COMMON PROBLEMS OF PRACTICE

Invariably, well-organized PLCs are keenly focused on specific student learning outcomes. Educators come together as a team and develop shared goals for student achievement, shared strategies to *get from here to there*, and shared evaluations of learners' progress. Teachers in high-powered PLCs regularly converse about student achievement data with specific aims in mind. For example, teachers can view samples of student work or video recorded examples of students engaged in problem solving. Pertinent discussions within a PLC meeting might concentrate on teaching strategies that supported and/or interfered with deep learning in these activities. Further, triangulation of data, from informal to standardized test measures is essential to construct valid interpretation of teaching effectiveness. Progressive changes within schools (i.e., reform and improvement tactics) representing best practices of learning communities include intensive crossover among curricula, assessment results, and academic standards (Darling-Hammond & Richardson, 2009; DuFour, DuFour, Eaker, & Karhanek, 2004: Hallam, Smith, Hite, Hite, & Wilcox, 2015; Knapp, 2003; Poskitt, 2014; Rentfro, 2007; Yoon, Duncan, Lee, Scarloss, & Shapley, 2007).

Administrators can help shape the culture and attitudes of teachers by emphasizing a big picture view of assessment and highlighting areas ripe for guilt-free collaborative change.

Reviewing student work with other teachers is a powerful strategy for improving instruction and student success. In order to be truly transformative, however, PLCs must demonstrate effective *use* of outcomes data. A school culture unafraid of examining student achievement data is well suited to begin the process of closely scrutinizing school successes and failures with an eye toward program enhancement. On the other hand, a school culture rife with fear of consequences for failure, is unsupportive of a reflective and productive PLC. Administrators can help shape the culture and attitudes of teachers by emphasizing a *big picture view* of assessment and highlighting areas ripe for *guilt-free* collaborative change. To be sure, teachers and school administrators may require additional training to make effective decisions about instructional modification informed by assessment data. Administrators can help shape the culture and attitudes of teachers by emphasizing a holistic view of assessment and highlighting areas ripe for guilt-free collaborative change. Once a positive framework is set, schools can begin to establish norms, agree upon common

PLC DISCUSSION TOPICS

Student Data

Reflection on Practice

Lesson Effectiveness

Grading Practices

Classroom Management

Policy Implementation

Unit Planning

Assessment Strategies

Peer-Observations

Questioning Techniques

Problems of Practice

Individual Needs

Extracurricular Enhancement

Enrichment Experiences

Teaching Methodologies

Curriculum Alignment

Parent Communication

Accountability Systems

appraisals, and design results-oriented instructional development. Shared terminology can evolve, for instance, in terms of levels of teacher questioning and sophistication of students' responses. From a practical standpoint, PLCs rely upon team agreement of student evaluation criteria, types of formative and summative assessments, and systematic interventions that impact higher student attainment of collective goals (Breyfogle & Spotts, 2011; DuFour, 2007; Hughes-Hassell, Brasfield, & Dupree, 2012; Ruddy & Prusinsky, 2012; Vescio, Ross, & Adams, 2007).

Another practical consideration and recommended best practice for PLCs is the inclusion of manageable tasks. Professional development activities should be embedded into scheduled meetings in a manner that allows teachers sufficient time to concentrate on specific learning goals. Practical tasks can include discussion of themed articles or books, choosing one or two targets for instructional improvement, video sharing, or analysis of other classroom data. PLC tasks need to be developed gradually upon reflection of school priorities. Tasks must be meaningful and are, ideally, drawn from cohesive content units. For instance, teachers might meet numerous times per year to evaluate student writing using state rubrics. Meetings may be scheduled face-to-face or through other means. Computer-mediated communication methods (CMC) offer manageable ways for teachers to communicate with peers in a prompt and effective manner. PLCs can utilize any number of technology-based methods for economizing team activities including discussion boards, chat rooms, wikis, and private social media groups. Best practices are geared toward functional application activities for teachers. Learning community activities can be both effective and accessible; offering strategies to implement in the classroom and exposing educators to new ideas from specialists. In addition, strong PLCs outline manageable tasks with varying levels of involvement; giving participants a chance to alternately (and creatively) present or observe depending on the shared goals for the session (Battersby & Verdi, 2015; Duncan-Howell, 2010; Holmes, 2013; Stahl, 2015).

Evidence exists supporting PLC exploration of issues that go beyond subject matter. To this end, meetings are recommended with a concentration on written reflections, student data, or other teacher-identified issues that affect school effectiveness. Tasks should be selected that facilitate brief assessment of student outcomes and active involvement in organizing straightforward follow-through and follow-up. Learning is *built in* to daily work by agreeing upon practices to try out, reflect upon, and bring back to the group for discussion (Attard, 2012; Sigudardottir, 2010).

RECCOMENDATION SIX

PROFESSIONAL LEARNNIG COMMUNITIES SHOULD INCLUDE

NON-EVALUATIVE PEER OBSERVATION

Numerous studies have found that peer observation is an effective method of professional growth (Daniels, Pirayoff, & Bessant, 2013; TNTP, 2014; TNTP, 2013; Hendry & Oliver, 2012; Eri, 2014; Bill and Melinda Gates Foundation, 2014). As such, it should be a primary activity for PLCs. School and classroom visits serve as catalysts for new ideas. When teachers are able to conduct multiple visits, they can be invigorated by witnessing a variety of teaching examples. Post-observation reviews and discussions provide opportunities for educators to plan and experiment with new instructional techniques (Berry, 2008; Darling-Hammond, 2008; Eri, 2014; Hendry & Oliver, 2012; LeClerc, et al., 2012; Little, 2006; The New Teacher Project, 2013).

Moreover, peer observations need not be narrowly viewed as exclusively focused on teacher behaviors. Observations give participants a window into the total classroom environment including student perspectives, ways to better support learning, specific teaching practices, and larger reflections on the teaching process. By reflecting on current teaching conventions, educators are able to debrief and gain added confidence from colleagues (Daniels, Pirayoff, & Bessant, 2013; Hendry & Oliver, 2012; The New Teacher Project, 2013).

Peer observations should be structured with reasonable expectations of observers. Teachers are not necessarily required to provide detailed feedback to each other; rating a laundry list of performance characteristics. Rather, observations, *in and of themselves* can have a huge impact on teaching. Watching other teachers in action leads to affirmation of valuable teaching methods and introduction to new methods. Teachers can model a particular lesson or approach to a concept, thereby assisting observers in developing self-efficacy, i.e., the belief in their ability to employ fresh strategies. Observers are in a unique position of being better able to analyze, in real time, the reactions of students to pedagogical practices and see themselves as capable of eliciting the same kinds of reactions. Debrief discussions following observations provide an opportunity for problem-solving without judgment or evaluation. Engaging in a collaborative observational undertaking has tremendous potential for strengthening and energizing classroom methodologies (Daniels, Pirayoff, & Bessant, 2013; Hendry & Oliver, 2012; The New Teacher Project, 2013).

Peer observations have also been shown to greatly impact the self-efficacy of participants through the power of vicarious experience. Bandura's theory of self-efficacy (1997) suggests that one's belief in his or her ability to succeed correlates to their actual levels of success. Vicarious experience, or observing the success of failures of someone in a similar situation, has been shown to greatly impact self-efficacy. This phenomenon has been studied many times through the lens of professional growth. Al-Awidi and Alghazo's work in 2012 demonstrate that student teachers who had vicariously experienced success utilizing new technologies were more likely to use the technology in their classrooms later. A similar study used video streamed experiences of students describing past successes and found that it boosted the confidence of adult learners who viewed them (Bartsch, Case, & Meerman, 2012).

RECCOMENDATION SEVEN

PROFESSIONAL LEARNING COMMUNITIES SHOULD HAVE ADEQUATE TIME AND SUPPORT

School administration plays a critical role in supporting teachers' dedication to engineering better collaborative models for instructional decision-making. PLCs must be provided with a solid organizational structure, sufficient time to develop new ideas and practices, and streamlined procedures for discussing pedagogical strategies. In other words, sound mechanisms that promote teacher learning need to be in place for PLCs to be successful (LeClerc, Moreau, Dumouchel, & Sallafranque-St.Louis, 2012; Letor, 2006).

A recent study by TNTP (2015) found that teachers, on average, spend 150 hours per year in professional learning situations. These could include workshops, conferences, or other forms or training. Professional learning delivered through the PLC model must be supported by providing adequate time to allow the many activities of the PLC to take place. For example, if a PLC is going to utilize peer observation as a tool for development, time must be created during the day for that group of teachers to conduct observations. Similarly, if student work is to be reviewed, time and flexibility must be provided for that work to be created, collected, and reviewed both individually and by the group.

Also, it is important that teachers have time to work together without having administration in the PLC. PLC members can have concerns they do not feel comfortable bringing up to administration. If the school leadership are involved in the PLC at every turn, teachers feel they do not have the trust of the administration. Being able to share concerns and problems is vital to teacher morale and effectiveness and frequently referred to as a key factor in teacher retention (Webb et al. 2009).

While participant ownership and autonomy is important, the role of the principal as a guiding factor cannot be ignored. In effective PLC groups, the administration aids the PLC by asking probing questions and offering outside support. The administration may have access to a knowledge base that is not directly available to the teachers, such as district wide data or assessment instruments or work samples for neighboring schools. By providing this outside information, the administrator(s) is(are) able to help the PLC reach their learning goals without interfering with their autonomous leadership (LeClerc, Moreau, Dumouchel, & Sallafranque-St.Louis, 2012).

REFERENCES

Al-Awidi, H.H., & Alghazo, I.A. (2012). The effect of student teaching experiences on preservice elementary teachers' self-efficacy beliefs for technology integration in the UAE. *Educational Technology Research & Development, 60(5),* 923-941.

Attard, K. (2012). Public reflection within learning communities: an incessant type of professional development. *European Journal of Teacher Education, 35,* 199-211.

Bandura, A. (1997). *Self-efficacy: The exercise of control.* New York: Freeman.

Bartsch, R.A., Case, K.A., & Meerman, H. (2012). Increasing academic self-efficacy in statistics with a live vicarious experience presentation. *Teaching Psychology 2012* 39:133.

Battersby, S.L. & Verdi, B. (2015). The culture of professional learning communities and connections to improve teacher efficacy and support student learning. *Arts Education Policy Review, 116,* 22-29.

Berry, D. (2008). Learning by observing our peers. *Collected Essays on Learning and Teaching, 1,* 99-103.

Breyfogle, M.L. & Spotts, B. (2011). Professional development delivered right to your door. *Teaching Children Mathematics, 17,* 420-426.

Chong, W.H. & Kong, C.A. (2012). Teacher collaborative learning and teacher self-efficacy: The case of lesson study. *Journal of Experimental Education, 80*(3). 263-283.

Daniels, E., Pirayoff, R. & Bessant, S. (2013). Using peer observation and collaboration to improve teaching practices. *Universal Journal of Educational Research, 1,* 268-274.

D'Ardenne, C., Barnes, D.G., Hightower, E.S., Lamason, P.R., Mason, M., Patterson, P.C., Stephens, N., Wilson, C.E., Smith, V.H., & Erickson, K.A. (2013). PLCs in action: Innovative teaching for struggling grade 3-5 readers. *The Reading Teacher, 67,* 143-151.

Darling-Hammond, L. (2008). Teacher learning that supports student learning. *Teaching for Intelligence, 2, 91-100.*

Darling-Hammond, L. & Richardson, N. (2009). Research review/teacher learning: What matters? *How Teachers Learn, 66,* 46-53.

Demir, K. (2015). The effect of organizational trust on the culture of teacher leadership in primary schools. *Educational Sciences: Theory and Practice, 15(3)* 621-634.

DuFour, R. (2004). What is a professional learning community? *Educational Leadership, 61,* 6-11.

DuFour, R. (2007). Professional learning communities: A bandwagon, an idea worth considering, or our best hope for high levels of learning? *Middle School Journal, 39,* 4-8.

DuFour, R. (2011). Work together but only if you want to. *Kappan, 92,* 57-61.

DuFour, R., DuFour, R., Eaker, R., & Karhanek, G. (2004). *Whatever it takes: How professional learning communities respond when kids don't learn.* Bloomington, IN: National Educational Service.

Dufour, R., Eaker R. (1988). *Professional learning communities at work: Best practices for enhancing student achievement.* Bloomington, IN: National Education Service.

Duncan-Howell, J. (2010). Teachers making connections: Online communities as a source of professional learning. *British Journal of Educational Technology, 41,* 324-340.

Eri, R. (2014). Peer observation of teaching: Reflections of an early career academic. *Universal Journal of Educational Research, 2,* 625-631.

Garet, M. S., Porter, A. C., Desimone, L., Birman, B. F., & Yoon, K. S. (2001). What makes professional development effective? Results from a national sample of teachers. *American Educational Research Journal, 38,* 915-945.

Gray, J., Kruse, S., & Tarter, C.J. (2016). Enabling school structures, collegial trust, and academic emphasis. *Educational Management Administration & Leadership, 44(6),* 875-891.

Grossman, P. L., Valencia, S. W., Evans, K., Thompson, C., Martin, S., & Place, N. (2000). Transitions into teaching: Learning to teach writing in teacher education and beyond. *Journal of Literacy Research, 32,* 631-662.

Hallam, P.R., Smith, H.R., Hite, J.M. Hite, S.J., & Wilcox, B.R. (2015). Trust and collaboration in PLC teams: Teacher relationships, principal support, and collaborative benefits. *NASSP Bulletin, 99, 193-216.*

Hargreaves, A. (2001). The emotional geographies of teachers' relations with colleagues. *International Journal of Educational Research, 35,* 503-527.

Hawley, W. D., & Valli, L. (1999). The essentials of effective professional development: A new consensus. *Teaching as the learning profession: Handbook of policy and practice,* 127-150.

Hendry, G.D., & Oliver, G.R. (2012). Seeing is believing: The benefits of peer observation. *Journal of University Teaching & Learning Practice, 9,* 1-9.

Hoaglund, A.E., Birkenfield, K., & Box, J.A. (2014). Professional learning communities: Creating a foundation for collaboration skills in pre-service teachers. *Education, 134,* 521-528.

Holmes, B. (2013). School teachers' continuous professional development in an online learning community: Lessons from a case study of an eTwinning Learning Event. *European Journal of Education, 48,* 97-112.

Hughes-Hassell, S., Brasfield, A., & Dupree, D. (2012). Making the most of professional learning communities. *Knowledge Quest, 41,* 30-37.

Ingvarson, L., Meiers, M., & Beavis, A. (2005). Factors affecting the impact of professional development programs on teachers' knowledge, practice, student outcomes & efficacy.

Johnson, C. C., Kahle, J. B., & Fargo, J. D. (2007). A study of the effect of sustained, whole-school professional development on student achievement in science. *Journal of Research in Science Teaching, 44,* 775-786.

Kallan, F. (2016). Relationship between professional learning community, bureaucratic structure and organizational trust in primary education schools. *Educational Sciences: Theory and Practice, 16(5)* 1619-1637.

Knapp, M. S. (2003). Professional development as a policy pathway. *Review of Research in Education, 27,* 109-

157.

Labianca, G., Gray, B., & Brass, D. J. (2000). A grounded model of organizational schema change during empowerment. *Organization Science, 11,* 235-257.

LeClerc, M., Moreau, A.C., Dumouchel, C., & Sallafranque-St.Louis, F. (2012). Factors that promote progression in schools functioning as professional learning community. *International Journal of Education Policy & Leadership, 7,* 1-14.

Lee, J. C. K., Zhang, Z., & Yin, H. (2011). A multilevel analysis of the impact of a professional learning community, faculty trust in colleagues and collective efficacy on teacher commitment to students. *Teaching and Teacher Education, 27,* 820-830.

Letor, C. (2006). Teachers' collaboration and knowledge management in a prescriptive and legal framework: An inquiry on organizational conditions. In *European Educational Research Association Congress.*

Little, J.W., (2006). Professional community and professional development in the learning-centered school. *National Education Association: Best Practices Working Paper.* Washington, DC: National Education Association.

Louis, K.S. (2006). Changing the culture of schools: Professional community, organizational learning, and trust. *Journal of School Leadership, 16,* 477-489.

MacBeath, J. (1999). Why schools must speak for themselves. *Education Review-London, 12,* 27-33.

Macbeath, J., & Mortimore, P. (2001). *Improving school effectiveness.* McGraw-Hill Education (UK).

MacGilchrist, B., Reed, J., & Myers, K. (2004). *The intelligent school.* Sage.

Morrissey, M. S. (2000). Professional learning communities: An ongoing exploration.

Ozdem, G. (2011). An analysis of the mission and vision statements of the strategic plans of higher education institutions. *Educational Sciences: Theory ?& Practice, 11*(4), 18878-1894.

Owen, S. (2014). Teacher professional learning communities: Going beyond contrived collegiality toward challenging debate and collegial learning and professional growth. *Australian Journal of Adult Learning, 54,* 54-77.

Poskitt, J. (2014). Transforming professional learning and practice in assessment for learning. *The Curriculum Journal, 25,* 542-566.

Prytula, M.P. (2012). Teacher metacognition within the professional learning community. *International Education Studies, 5,* 112-121.

Rentfro, E.R. (2007). Professional learning communities impact student success. *Leadership Compass, 5, 1-3.*

Rosenholtz, S. J., Bassler, O., & Hoover-Dempsey, K. (1986). Organizational conditions of teacher learning. *Teaching and Teacher Education, 2*(2), 91-104.

Ruddy, A. and Prusinsky, E. (2012). Professional development for school improvement: The case of Indiana. *Journal of School Leadership, 22,* 55-78.

Schrum, L., & Levin, B. B. (2013). Leadership for twenty-first-century schools and student achievement: lessons learned from three exemplary cases. *International Journal of Leadership in Education, 16,* 379-398.

Shen, J., Zhen, J., & Poppink, S. (2007). Open lessons: A practice to develop a learning community for teachers. *Educational Horizons, 85,* 181-191.

Siguδardottir, A.K. (2010). Professional learning community in relation to school effectiveness. *Scandinavian Journal of Educational Research, 54,* 395-412.

Stahl, K. A. (2015). Using professional learning communities to bolster comprehension instruction. *The Reading Teacher, 68,* 327-333.

Stein, M. K., Smith, M. S., & Silver, E. (1999). The development of professional developers: Learning to assist teachers in new settings in new ways. *Harvard Educational Review, 69,* 237-270.

Stoll, L., Bolam, R., McMahon, A., Wallace, M., & Thomas, S. (2006). Professional learning communities: A review of the literature. *Journal of Educational Change, 7,* 221-258.

TNTP (2013). *Fixing classroom observations: How common core will change the way we look at teaching.* New York, NY: Author.

TNTP (2015). The Mirage: Confronting the hard truth about our quest for teacher development. New York, NY: Author.

Vann, B.A., & Hinton, B.E. (1994). *Workplace social networks and their relationship to student retention in on-site ged programs.* Human Resource Development Quarterly, 5: 141-151.

Vann, B.A. (1996). *Learning self-direction in a social and experimental context.* Human Resource Development Quarterly, 7: 121-130.

Vescio, V., Ross, D., & Adams, A. (2007). A review of research on the impact of professional learning communities on teaching practice and student learning. *Teaching and Teacher Education, 24,* 80-91.

Villa, C. (2003). Community building to serve all students. *Education, 123*(4), 777.

Wells, C. & Feun, L. (2007). Implementation of learning community principles: A study of six high schools. *NASSP Bulletin, 91,* 141-160.

Yoon, K. S., Duncan, T., & Lee, S., WY., Scarloss, B., & Shapley, K.(2007). *Reviewing the evidence on how teacher professional development affects student achievement.* (Issues & Answers Report, REL 2007–No. 033). Washington, DC: U.S. Department of Education, Institute of Education Sciences, National Center for Education Evaluation and Regional Assistance, Regional Educational Laboratory Southwest.

The Bluegrass Center for Teacher Quality is a 501(c)(3) nonprofit organization based out of Kentucky. The Mission of the Bluegrass Center for Teacher Quality is to provide high quality, research based professional learning opportunities to teachers in Kentucky. We will accomplish this goal by: (1) empowering educators to take ownership of their knowledge and share that knowledge with others, (2) facilitating school wide programs designed to usher in positive, lasting change in a school (3) developing new models for professional development and researching new adult learning strategies, and (4) advocating for positive reform movements that make professional learning more readily available to all school staff. You can learn more about the Bluegrass Center for Teacher Quality at www.bgteacherquality.org.

ABOUT THE AUTHORS

Matthew B. Courtney, Ed.D.

Dr. Matthew B. Courtney is the Founder and Volunteer Executive Director of the Bluegrass Center for Teacher Quality. As a music teacher, Dr. Courtney struggled to find meaningful ways to grow professionally. Professional learning opportunities were limited and quality was low. Dr. Courtney left the classroom in 2013 to start the Bluegrass Center for Teacher Quality. Through the Center, Dr. Courtney has studied professional learning in both theoretical and practical applications. His *Master Teacher Network* model of professional learning earned national attention in 2014 when it was held up by Secretary of Education Arne Duncan as an example of the future of teacher leadership. Dr. Courtney is dedicated to uncovering new and powerful ways to ensure the continued professional growth of teachers across Kentucky. His research includes creating and piloting new models, and seeking to improve existing tools.

Joseph Constantine, Ph.D., CCC-SLP

Dr. Joseph Constantine is an Assistant Professor of Speech-Language Pathology at Eastern Kentucky University. He received his Ph.D. in Education, Childhood Language Arts, and Reading and M.S. in Speech-Language Pathology from the University of South Florida. He is a licensed & certified speech-language pathologist. Dr. Constantine has more than 20 years of experience teaching pre-service educators to work with learning disabilities including helping students with language impairments, reading and writing challenges, social communication issues, and behavior problems. His educational philosophy is based upon student-centered theories of learning. He has been responsible for developing a number of innovative educational programs for young children as well as teens and adult learners. With an eye toward ameliorating interventions for at-risk students in public school settings, Dr. Constantine has dedicated his professional career to *building a better safety net* for students with learning difficulties. He has developed a unique blend of cognitive-behavioral and communication-oriented strategies to effect positive changes in schools that address both social-emotional and academic needs of students. Dr. Constantine regularly provides community lectures and workshops for teachers and parents on a variety of topics in education. He is a committed advocate for best practices and improved educational supports for children and young adults.

Joshua Trosper, M.Ed.

Mr. Joshua Trosper is an Assistant Principal at Knox Central High School in Barbourville, Kentucky. He received his Master of Arts in Educational Leadership from Union College and Bachelor of Science in Elementary Education from Campbellsville University. Mr. Trosper has experience teaching from Kindergarten to 5th Grade. His administrative experience spans from 4 and a half years at the elementary/middle level and is in his first year at the high school level. With such a diverse education background, Mr. Trosper has a wealth of experience working with teachers. He has led professional development sessions on a broad spectrum of education issues from School Safety, Building Relationships and Education Evaluation System tips. He is a tireless advocate for teacher leadership and professional growth.

Peer Review Committee

This guidebook was reviewed and approved by an independent peer review committee.

- Jason Reeves, Ed.D. – Dean of Education, Union College
- Donna Spencer Pitts, Ph.D. – Assistant Professsor, Eastern Kentucky University
- Tara Isaacs, Ph.D. – Coordinator, Professional & Deeper Learning Academic Services, Jefferson County Public Schools

Notes:

Notes:

Notes:

Notes:

www.ingramcontent.com/pod-product-compliance
Lightning Source LLC
Chambersburg PA
CBHW081143280526
45787CB00007B/3208